W9-CDX-999

What Was the Plague?

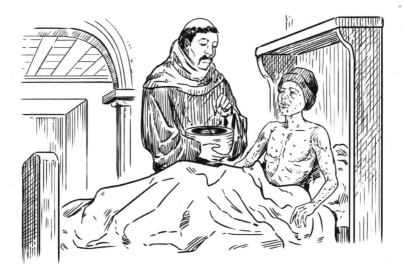

by Roberta Edwards

illustrated by Dede Putra

Penguin Workshop

PENGUIN WORKSHOP
An imprint of Penguin Random House LLC, New York

First published in the United States of America by Penguin Workshop,
an imprint of Penguin Random House LLC, New York, 2021

Copyright © 2021 by Penguin Random House LLC

Penguin supports copyright. Copyright fuels creativity, encourages diverse voices,
promotes free speech, and creates a vibrant culture. Thank you for buying an authorized
edition of this book and for complying with copyright laws by not reproducing, scanning,
or distributing any part of it in any form without permission. You are supporting writers
and allowing Penguin to continue to publish books for every reader.

PENGUIN is a registered trademark and PENGUIN WORKSHOP is a trademark
of Penguin Books Ltd. WHO HQ & Design is a registered trademark
of Penguin Random House LLC.

Visit us online at penguinrandomhouse.com.

Library of Congress Cataloging-in-Publication Data is available.

Printed in the United States of America

ISBN 9780593383650 (paperback)   10 9 8 7 6 5 4 3 2 1 WOR
ISBN 9780593383667 (library binding)   10 9 8 7 6 5 4 3 2 1 WOR

Contents

What Was the Plague?

Looking back at history, certain periods stand out as times of progress and prosperity, when people enjoyed a better life than the generations before them had.

The three hundred years from 1000 to 1300 in Europe count as one of those prosperous periods. One reason is that there were not many wars. That meant kings, lords, and knights weren't off on battlefields and could stay at home in their manors or castles. There, along with noble ladies in rich gowns and headdresses, they could enjoy lavish feasts, often with music and acrobats. Together, they went off hunting deer. They enjoyed playing card games and chess, both of which had originated in the Far East.

Knights who served as soldiers for a lord kept up their battle skills through festive "pretend battles" called tournaments. In a contest called a joust, two knights in full armor on horseback would gallop straight at each other, each trying to knock his opponent off his horse with a hard blow from a lance. After showing off such strength

and bravery, the winner might get a keepsake from the lady he loved, who'd been sitting in the grandstand.

The peasants who farmed the lords' land had none of the luxuries enjoyed by the nobility. Nevertheless, they saw their lives improve, too. Because of certain inventions, the work of peasants was made easier. There were better plows to till the soil. A work harness designed for horses meant that peasants no longer had to depend on slow oxen to pull a plow. Ways of farming also improved. Varying what was grown and leaving part of the land fallow (unplanted) resulted in much bigger crops. That resulted in more food and, in turn, more food meant healthier people who no longer owed as much free labor to the lords, as had been the case in earlier times.

By the year 1300, the cities growing all over

Europe gave rise to a new middle class. These were people who had thriving businesses. In the social order, they fell in between the nobles at the top and the peasants at the bottom. There were guilds (groups of people all in the same type of business) producing high-quality goods—leather shoes, steel suits of armor, wooden furniture, and jewelry made from gold and silver. Trade was showing the first sign of becoming global, with ships connecting all the parts of the world known to Europe.

Western Europe was so prosperous that its population almost doubled between 1000 and 1300. Three cities—Paris, Milan, and Granada—each had 150,000 people living in them. Both Florence and Venice could claim a population of 100,000, and while London only had 80,000, it was growing into the most important trade center in Northern Europe.

To many, it must have seemed as if the good times would last forever. No one had cause to think that a disaster was coming. But one was.

About one-third of the population of Western Europe—an estimated twenty-five million people—was wiped out between 1345 and 1351. All because of tiny, disease-carrying fleas. The disease was called different names: the great mortality, the pestilence, and the black death. (Often, sick people's hands, feet, and mouths would turn black. It was that horrible.)

Today, this disease is most often called the plague. The people who managed to survive the plague faced a world that had been changed in almost unimaginable ways.

CHAPTER 1
You Definitely Have the Plague If . . .

The outbreak of the plague that started in 1345 and fizzled out in 1351 managed to reach much of the world known to Europeans at the time. It swept from China all the way west to Spain, and it went from Egypt as far north as the British Isles, Scandinavia, and Russia. When a disease spreads over many countries or continents, it is known as a pandemic.

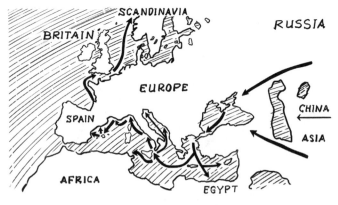

Spread of the plague in the 1300s

This pandemic of the plague killed a greater percentage of people than any other natural event in history. In the early 1300s, the total population of Western Europe had risen to about seventy-five million people. The best guess is that at least a third of them died. That's twenty-five million people. Some historians who have studied the disease think even this enormous number is too low—they say that as many as thirty-five million to forty-five million people may have died.

The plague pandemic was actually made up of three different kinds of the same disease. The disease was caused by a deadly germ. But unfortunately not even the most well-trained physicians in the Middle Ages had any knowledge of germs or how they spread. As for a cure, that had to wait for another six hundred years.

The least deadly form was the bubonic plague. (*Bubonic* meant the victims had lumpy sores called buboes.) It struck a person's lymph nodes, which are located in the neck, underarms, and inner thighs. Normally, lymph nodes work to fight against disease. But when infected with the plague, the lymph nodes turned dark and became swollen with pus.

Having a bubo was very painful. If a person had a large bubo on their neck, the only way to find relief from the pain was to tilt their head to the side and stay that way. Besides the buboes, a person would develop fever, chills, and dark splotches on the skin of their chest and back. They would vomit and have diarrhea.

Boo-Boos

The large purple egg-shaped bumps that appeared on nearly all victims of the plague were called buboes (say: BOO-boze). Today, when little children get a scrape, they might call it an "owie" or a "boo-boo." The word *boo-boo* actually comes from the plague-era buboes.

As if that weren't enough, the bubonic plague made victims smell awful and have terrible breath. Symptoms didn't appear for about five days. The only "plus" regarding the bubonic plague was that about 40 percent of people survived it.

Sometimes, the germ causing the plague spread from the lymph nodes to the lungs. This led to the second form of the plague: pneumonic (say: new-MOHN-nick) plague. *Pneumo* is the root of the Greek word for lungs.

Victims of the pneumonic plague coughed up blood and vomited constantly. They died within three days after they started coughing.

Only about one person out of twenty survived the pneumonic plague.

The third kind of the plague was the worst. *Nobody* survived the septicemic (say: sep-tuh-SEE-mick) plague. It occurred when the plague germs were able to enter a person's bloodstream, sending them to all parts of the body. This turned the skin around the mouth, nose, and hands of the victim black. The septicemic plague killed swiftly—in less than a day! There are stories of people who went to sleep feeling healthy but were dead by morning, as well as doctors who visited a person who was very sick with the plague and ended up dying even before their patient did.

Nosegays

People who lived through the plague and wrote about it always mentioned the terrible odor of its victims—their breath, their bodies, and the air around them. This was why people often carried bunches of flowers called nosegays with them. When held to their noses, the flowers helped hide the awful smells. Some people even believed nosegays could protect them from the plague—but that was just wishful thinking.

CHAPTER 2
When It Began

The pandemic that started in 1345 was the worst but not the first time the plague had wiped out much of the world. The period during the late 1340s is called the Second Pandemic because there had been a huge one much earlier. It lasted from 541 until 544. And there was a later pandemic in the 1890s. What all three pandemics have in common is that they originated in China.

The First Pandemic arrived during the rule of an emperor named Justinian I, so it is called the Justinian Plague. Justinian I ruled over a vast area known as the Byzantine Empire— southern Europe, the Middle East, and North Africa. The plague first hit Ethiopia and then

Egypt. From Africa, it spread to the Middle East before making its way into Europe. In the end, the First Pandemic struck all the countries surrounding the Mediterranean Sea. At Justinian I's beautiful capital of Constantinople (present-day Istanbul in Turkey), it is believed that the plague broke out after ships arrived carrying a large supply of grain from Egypt.

Byzantine Empire under Justinian I

(In Egypt, granaries—storage places for grain—were full of rats.) Justinian I himself did not escape the plague, which, at its peak, killed at least five thousand people—perhaps as many as ten thousand—a day.

Justinian the Great (482–565)

Justinian I was born Petrus Sabbatius in what is now Macedonia. Although he came from a peasant family, Justinian I received a good education and was trained to be a soldier. Through an important and powerful uncle, Justinian I came to rule over the vast Byzantine Empire from 527 to 565.

During his long reign as emperor, he had several major cathedrals built in the capital city (present-day Istanbul). The most famous is the Hagia Sophia, which today serves as a mosque for Muslim worshippers.

A historian named Procopius witnessed the plague in Constantinople. In a book called *Secret History*, he reported that so many people died, bodies were often left outside, and the whole city smelled of death. In the countryside, the plague was "wiping out most of the farming community." But even then, Justinian I kept demanding the yearly tax on every person still living.

Procopius was no fan of Justinian I's. He blamed the plague on the emperor who, he claimed, must have angered the gods. One-quarter of the Byzantine Empire's population is believed to have died within three years. However, there was no sudden end; outbreaks of the plague continued in the Mediterranean area for more than two hundred years, finally ending in 750.

The Third Pandemic originated much later, in southwest China. By 1894, it appeared in the Chinese city of Canton, a major trading port. By this time, merchant ships had been making ocean crossings for well over two hundred years. Ships spread the disease to Japan,

the island of Taiwan, Singapore, India, the coasts of North Africa and South America, Hawaii, and all the way to the coast of California and as far south as Sydney, Australia. It reached Europe in 1896, with cases in London and other port cities.

Spread of the Third Pandemic

The Third Pandemic is estimated to have killed fifteen million people. That's a terrible number but still far fewer than the two previous pandemics. Why? There may have been a much smaller population of rats by that time. Another likely reason is a better standard of living. Public-health measures meant cleaner streets, trash cans for garbage, and wagons to collect it. There were modern sewer systems, and hospitals where patients could remain isolated from others, preventing further spread of the disease. (In the Middle Ages, hospitals were places where people went to die, not to be healed.)

By the turn of the twentieth century, personal hygiene had improved greatly—people bathed more frequently, clothes were washed more often, and disinfectants were used to clean homes. Still, the Third Pandemic didn't go away for good until the 1940s when—at long last!—antibiotics were developed to treat those sick with the plague.

Are there still cases of the plague today? Yes, but a very small number. (The United States averages seven cases a year; one woman there contracted the plague after accidentally mowing down a diseased squirrel in her yard!) Antibiotics cure the disease, and there is now a vaccine to prevent the plague. The United States, however, does not keep supplies of the vaccine on hand because health officials say it's just not necessary.

Ring Around the Rosie

According to legend, the popular children's rhyme "Ring Around the Rosie" originally described the plague.

It seems so playful and innocent—everyone holds hands and moves in a circle, chanting the words until the end of the last line when "we all fall down." This is what the rhyme is really about:

"Ring, a ring, o'roses": The red rash that sometimes appeared with the plague.

"Pocket full of posies": Posies are flowers in the nosegays people carried, believing their sweet smell might prevent the plague.

"Ashes, ashes" or sometimes "A-tishoo! A-tishoo!": Both the sound of sneezing and coughing, symptoms of the pneumonic plague.

"We all fall down": This meant everyone fell down dead.

CHAPTER 3
Y. pestis—A Deadly Pest

Rats—specifically black rats—are often blamed as the cause for the black death. They certainly did a great job spreading it. Rats are responsible for the disease reaching all of Europe in only about three years during the late 1340s. But rats were actually plague victims themselves.

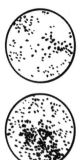

The bacterium *Yersinia pestis* is the real culprit.

In the 1890s, during the Third Pandemic ravaging China and India, scientists from many countries were determined to learn, once and for all, what was causing it. Each wanted to be first to find the answer.

The discovery was made by a young man named Alexandre Yersin. In 1894, Yersin was living in Hong Kong, where he carefully and closely examined the buboes of plague victims. Using a microscope, he saw short, stubby single-celled bacteria. Not many types of bacteria cause disease. In fact, certain types prevent disease, such as some in the stomach. But the ones Yersin found were deadly.

Alexandre Yersin

Because of his discovery, he received the honor of having the bacterium in buboes named after him. The Y in *Y. pestis* stands for Yersin.

Y. pestis exists in the stomach of a certain kind of flea—the rat flea. The rat flea is brown and very small. The biggest ones are no more than a quarter of an inch long. Rat fleas get their name

A rat flea

because they like to make their homes in the fur of black rats. The trouble starts as soon as a rat flea with *Y. pestis* bites a rat and drinks its blood. Now the rat is infected

with *Y. pestis*. If a flea on that rat bites a human being, then that person will get the plague.

As soon as rats carrying *Y. pestis* die, they are no longer a food source for rat fleas, which then move on to live rats. Often, one rat has many rat fleas on it—sometimes in the hundreds. Fleas move from rat to rat, continuing to feed on their blood. In this way, the number of rats with *Y. pestis* increases. They are now plague carriers, too.

Sometimes a rat flea doesn't find a rat anywhere nearby. Then it will spread the plague by jumping directly onto a human being. Rat fleas, however, prefer rats. Biting humans is not their first choice!

The plague struck down rich and poor, old and young. However, historians think that only about 25 percent of medieval nobility died of the plague in comparison to 40 percent of priests (who were often tending to the sick) and about 70 percent of poor peasant farmers and city laborers.

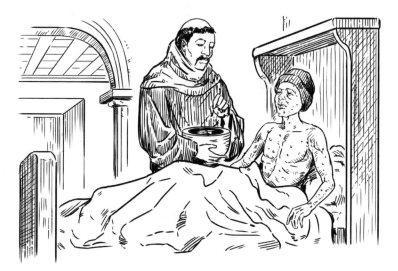

Rats! Everywhere, Rats

Rats were a common sight in the villages, towns, and cities of medieval Europe. People threw garbage and their own human waste right into the streets. Towns were dirty. All this was a feast for plague-carrying rats.

Rats would scurry inside houses. Then the fleas that traveled in on them would leap into people's straw mattresses and onto their clothing. Rats are good climbers, so they also could get inside walls and roofs.

Villages out in the countryside also had large populations of rats. Houses made of wattle and daub often had cracks and holes, making them easy to enter. (Wattle involves weaving twigs around the house's wood frame and covering it with daub, a mixture of straw, clay, and cow manure.) Luckier were the rich, whose large homes were built of stone, making it harder for flea-carrying rats to gain entry.

Can people with the plague give the disease directly to other people?

The answer is yes and no. Of the three kinds of plague, two do not spread from person to person: the bubonic plague and the septicemic plague. Just standing somewhere near a victim of either of those types would not pass the plague to someone else.

The pneumonic plague is different, however. A victim with the pneumonic plague coughs up droplets of blood that remain in the air awhile.

Another person close by can breathe in those droplets and catch the pneumonic plague. Think of how, by sneezing and coughing, a cold sufferer can pass the cold to others.

The good news is that the bacterium *Y. pestis* is not always around. These organisms hide underground, often for hundreds of years. Also, since the discovery of new medicines in the 1940s, any cases that do appear (approximately one to two thousand a year) are very treatable.

CHAPTER 4
The Plague Begins Its Journey

Most historians agree that the Second Pandemic of the plague started somewhere in inner Asia around 1345. It might have been in the Gobi Desert or near a lake close to the northwest border of China. What's certain is that the increase in trading between different parts of the world brought the disease from the Far East to Western Europe.

Rich people, especially those living in big cities such as Florence, Italy; Paris, France; and London, England, were increasingly eager for the silks, jewels, spices, and other luxury goods imported from China and India.

Merchants traveled from the Far East by land across the Gobi Desert and over great stretches

of grasslands to reach a midpoint port city. From there, ships would be loaded with the precious cargo and travel to cities in Europe where everything on board would be sold.

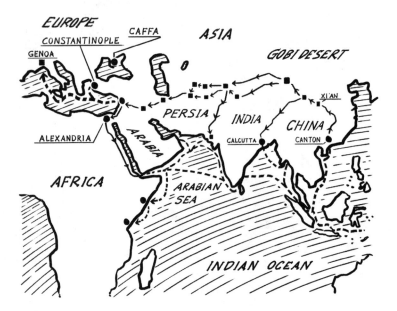

Fourteenth-century trade routes

Caffa, on the Black Sea, was one such port city. Although controlled by powerful merchants from Genoa, Italy, Caffa was actually part of the great Mongol empire. By the mid 1340s, the Mongol khan (emperor) decided to take back Caffa from the Genoese. However, by the time the Mongol army reached the outskirts of the walled city, some soldiers were falling sick and dying . . . of the plague.

Nevertheless, the Mongols did not retreat. They besieged the city from outside its walls. Instead of burying plague-ridden soldiers, the Mongol army turned the corpses into weapons. Loaded onto catapults, dead bodies were hurled inside the walls of Caffa.

The Genoese in Caffa had already heard about the terrible illness coming from the east. They realized what the Mongol soldiers had died from. Fearing that they would catch the plague from the corpses, many sailed away from Caffa, heading for home as fast as they could.

Unfortunately, some sailors aboard the Genoese ships had already become infected. Historical records are not in agreement as to the number of ships leaving Caffa—it may have been as many as twelve—or how many infected

crewmen were aboard each ship. En route to Genoa, the ships landed in Messina, a city on the island of Sicily right off the coast of Italy. By this time, some sailors were sick, and some had already died.

Messina was a popular stopover for merchant ships. The crewmen who still felt well probably hoped to rest up for a couple of days and pick up supplies before continuing on the last leg of their voyage up the coast of Italy. So they docked their ships in the harbor. A man from Messina spotted a friend on the deck of one of the Genoese ships. He invited him to his home. His friendly gesture allowed the plague to enter the city, the beginning of the pandemic that was to devastate Western Europe.

It was October 1347.

Other people from Messina, upon seeing dead sailors on the ships, were not so welcoming. They forced the group of Genoese boats to leave immediately in the hope that doing so would keep the plague away from their city. They didn't know it was already there.

Almost immediately, people in Messina began to fall sick and die. There are descriptions from

that time of people vomiting and coughing up blood. It sounds as if they were struck by the contagious pneumonic plague. It killed so many, so swiftly that soon pet dogs were roaming wild in the deserted streets.

Among those still living, many were too terrified to even care for family members. According to a man from Messina named Michele da Piazza, if a son got sick, "his father flatly refused to stay with him." By the fall of 1348, about a third of the whole population—not just of Messina, but all of Sicily—was wiped out.

Saint Roch

Not all people abandoned victims of the plague. Some behaved with great kindness. According to legend, in the fourteenth century, a Frenchman named Roch (say: rock) came upon a group of very sick people. They were dying of the plague. Instead of passing them by as others had, Roch stayed and did his best to help and comfort them.

He had known that by tending to these plague victims, he might catch the sickness. And he did. In order not to infect anyone else, Roch stayed hidden in the woods. Most likely, he thought he would die. However, a dog from a nearby village found Roch and began bringing him food every day.

Amazingly, Roch got better and returned home to France. Because of his kindness to the plague-ridden people, the church later made him a saint—a special holy person. By the 1500s, there were statues of Saint Roch in many churches in Northern France. People would come and pray before a statue of Saint Roch, hoping that he would help cure sick people in their own families.

CHAPTER 5
To Italy and Beyond

The remaining crews on the Genoese ships sailed on to various port cities on the west coast of Italy. This meant the plague had now reached

the mainland of Europe, and it began to travel inland. There was no stopping it. Because news of the plague was spreading as fast as the disease itself, flaming arrows were sometimes shot directly at the ships to prevent them from entering a harbor. In each location, it took about seven to nine months before the plague moved to another city.

The map below shows the various routes the black death took. Following one path, it traveled from Italy to France, reaching the city of Marseille by February 1348. It continued farther west into Spain and up through France, hitting the city of Avignon in March, reaching Paris sometime that summer, and crossing into England from Calais via the English Channel.

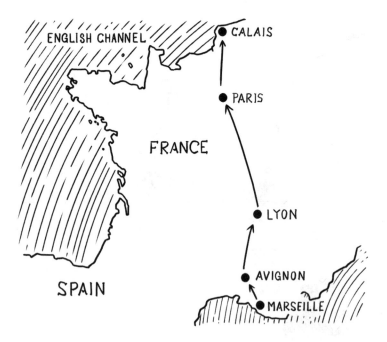

Path of the plague from Italy to Paris, France

Another path also started in Italy. It headed north over the Alps into Switzerland, where it veered off into Germany and regions around the Rhine River. Yet another route crossed the Mediterranean Sea into Egypt. Sometimes, the plague was able to travel two and a half miles a day! By 1349, it had reached as far north as Scandinavia and parts of Russia.

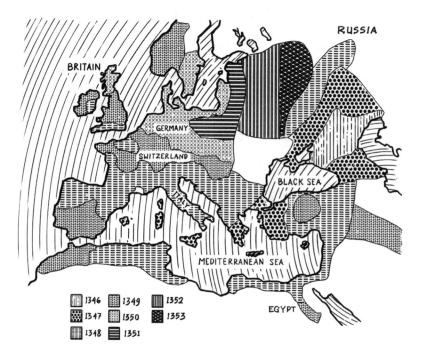

Path of the plague from Italy to Scandinavia

The Ghost Ship

The northern European region of Scandinavia is made up of present-day Denmark, Sweden, and Norway. Because it lies far north on the Baltic Sea, Scandinavians hoped that the black death might never reach their shores. Then one day, a ship was spotted drifting offshore near the town of Bergen, Norway. Soon it ran aground in the harbor. When some brave people went aboard to inspect the ship, they found a cargo of woolen cloth and lots of flea-infested rats. As for the crew—each and every man was dead. From the plague.

Certain cities, such as Milan, Italy; Liege, France; and Nuremburg, Germany, were spared the worst of the pandemic. However, some towns were practically wiped out, with 90 percent of their people gone. In England, some towns were left deserted, the few survivors having fled. In time, their ruins became overgrown and disappeared. Today, they can only be seen from airplanes overhead.

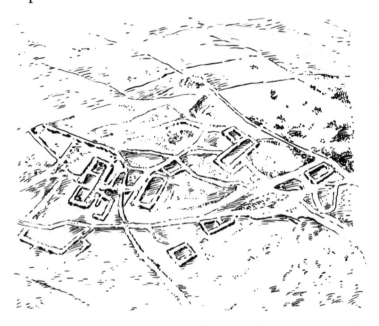

Deserted English village of Hound Tor

Burying all the dead became a horrible problem. Once church cemeteries filled up, plague victims had to be buried in mass graves.

A deep pit was dug. Then gravediggers laid a row of bodies across the bottom of the pit and covered them with a thin layer of dirt. Then another row of bodies was added to the pit, again topped by dirt. And so it went, until there were five layers of bodies and the pit became

full. A man from Siena, Italy, was not trying to make a joke when he described the process as similar to making lasagna. When there was no more public land in Avignon, France, to turn into burial pits, bodies were dumped right into the Rhône River.

The plague killed off so many that cities and towns would reach a point where there were no more priests to say prayers for the dying. As more and more gravediggers died from the plague, those that remained charged higher and higher fees for their services. When no gravediggers were left, family members had to bury their dead themselves.

Agnolo di Tura, from Siena, wrote, "No one could be found to bury the dead for money or for friendship. . . . And I, Agnolo di Tura, called the Fat, buried my five children with my own hands and so did many others likewise." Often, corpses lay rotting in houses or on the streets, where they were prey to wild dogs.

Describing what living through the plague years was like, another man from Siena summed it up when he wrote, "Almost everyone expected death. . . . People said and believed, 'This is the end of the world.'"

CHAPTER 6
A Medieval Medical Degree

When the plague hit Paris, France, in 1348, the people there had hope that victims might be saved. That was because Paris had one of the oldest and most famous universities. It specialized in teaching medicine. Some of the best doctors of the time had studied there and still remained in Paris, both teaching and tending to patients.

University of Paris in the Middle Ages

Doctors in the Middle Ages tended to the rich and were well-respected members of their communities. They dressed in expensive clothes to show off their importance—long red or purple robes with fur-trimmed hoods. Some even wore gold spurs when they rode on horseback to visit patients. But they did *not* wear large, dramatic masks.

Plague Doctors

There are very old prints of "plague doctors" wearing wide-brimmed hats, small spectacles, and strange masks with a large bird beak. (In certain European cities, such as Venice, souvenir shops still sell copies of these masks to tourists.) But during the Second Pandemic, doctors did not wear such masks. A sixteenth-century doctor created the first one, two hundred years after the Second Pandemic. The beak was filled with crushed flowers and sweet-smelling spices.

Even doctors with degrees from the best universities knew nothing about the true causes of diseases like the plague. As amazing as it may seem to modern readers, the study of medieval

Galen

medicine rested on beliefs about disease that were already more than 1,500 years old! These beliefs came from the teachings of Galen of ancient Rome and Hippocrates from ancient Greece. They are still considered by historians to be among the very first "doctors." Their ideas continued to be taught to medical students of the Middle Ages and after.

Doctors-to-be listened to lectures but, unlike today's medical students, they did not study the human body by actually cutting open a cadaver (a dead body) to study it. This was because the Christian church considered it sinful and disrespectful to a human body. At best, medical students observed the insides of a cadaver once every two years.

Hippocrates

According to the medicine of the Middle Ages, the human body was made up of four substances called humors. And, by the way, the humors had nothing to do with anything funny! There was black bile, yellow bile, blood, and phlegm (say: flem). Bile is made, in part, of acids and salts that help with digestion. Phlegm is the thick, goopy stuff you cough up from your throat and lungs when you're sick.

Hippocrates and Galen

Hippocrates lived from about 460 BC to about 375 BC. That is more than 2,400 years ago. He is often called the father of medicine. He taught students that diseases came from an unhealthy diet. In other words, he was saying that natural causes led to sickness.

Hippocrates teaching his students

This was at a time when people believed that they got sick because one of the many Greek gods was angry with them. He also set forth a theory (an idea that tries to explain how something works) about the importance of four substances in the body (called humors) and how they affected a person's health.

Galen was born into a rich Greek family in AD 129. He grew up in the city of Pergamon, in present-day Turkey. Later, he moved to Rome, where he was the physician of several emperors. He believed in the theory of four humors as explained by Hippocrates. He also believed in studying the insides of animal bodies—he worked on dead monkeys, for instance, and dead pigs—to gain a better understanding of how all the different organs worked. This was the beginning of the science of anatomy.

Galen dissecting a monkey

Each humor controlled a different part of the body. The most important thing was for a person's four humors to stay balanced. If they were, all the different organs in the body—the heart, the lungs, the stomach—would work properly. If there were too much of one humor in the body, a person would get sick.

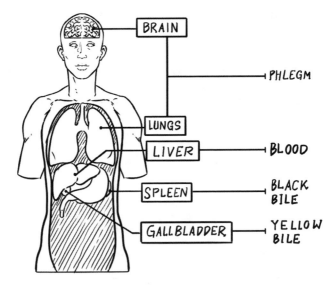

It was believed that the humors could also influence someone's personality. For instance, a person with a lot of yellow bile was thought to grow angry very easily. A person who was often sad supposedly had a lot of black bile, according to medieval doctors. This kind of person often was also artistic. A lot of phlegm caused people to be fair, calm, thoughtful, and ready to settle an argument through compromise. They were also known to be hardworking people. People who were happy and friendly were thought to have a large amount of blood in their body.

yellow bile

black bile

phlegm

blood

As students, future doctors learned everything there was to know about the four humors. They also learned how to perform certain kinds of surgery. How long they studied depended on which university they were training at. An average was about seven years.

Medical doctors performed surgeries, but so did men with no university training. They were known as ordinary surgeons. They often operated on soldiers at a battlefield. If a soldier got shot in the leg with an arrow, there was a good chance he could die from infection. To prevent that, a surgeon cut off the soldier's leg above the wound and closed the stump by cauterizing it (that meant quickly burning the wound to seal it). Off the battlefield, these medieval surgeons were barbers. That's why barber poles to this day have red stripes, signifying all the blood once spilled by barbers during the surgeries and other medical procedures they performed!

Sometimes the most effective help for the sick came from people with no training at all. In Western Europe at that time, 90 percent of

the population lived in the countryside in small villages with perhaps only a hundred people. Still, almost every village had a "healer"—usually an elderly woman, living alone.

These women often helped pregnant women deliver their babies. And on their own, they studied how herbs and plants might either cure illness or at least ease pain. From their gardens,

these healers made medicines. For instance, sage was used to help get rid of a headache. A mixture of licorice and comfrey might cure a cough.

Sometimes these remedies really did the job. Even today, many cough medicines contain licorice. However, even the most knowledgeable healers never came up with a cure for the plague.

CHAPTER 7
Curious Cures

So, if a person became sick, how did a trained doctor in the Middle Ages try to treat them?

First, they would examine a patient, looking to see if they had a fever and if the color of their skin appeared too pale or too flushed—too red.

They would ask about the patient's diet—were they eating healthy foods? And like doctors today, they'd ask a patient what was bothering them. Did their stomach hurt? Was their throat sore?

Richard T. Nowitz/The Image Bank/Getty Images

Justinian I (center), Byzantine emperor
during the First Pandemic, in 541

Rats were one of the primary spreaders of the Second Pandemic.

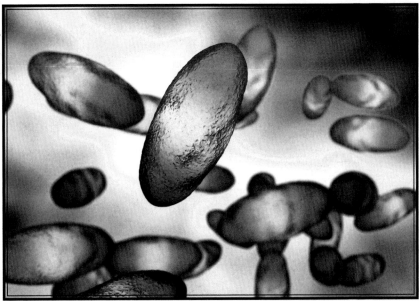

The plague bacterium, *Yersinia pestis*, which
was discovered by Alexandre Yersin

Nigel Hicks/The Image Bank/Getty Images

The remains of Hound Tor, an English village abandoned
in the mid-1300s, likely because of the plague

Timothy Allen/Stone/Getty Images

Trade routes during the plague in the 1300s
crossed the Gobi Desert in inner Asia.

An engraving of plague victims being buried together in mass graves

This beaked mask is often falsely associated with the black death but was not created until about two hundred years after the Second Pandemic.

iiJacker/iStock/Getty Images

Poet and writer Giovanni Boccaccio (1313–1375) wrote the
Decameron about ten people trying to avoid the plague.

wynnter/iStock/Getty Images

A medieval doctor from the 1400s presents medicine to a patient.

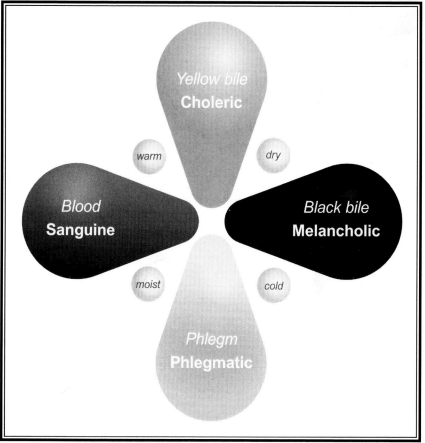

PeterHermesFurian/iStock/Getty Images

The bodily humors—yellow bile, black bile, phlegm, and blood

The Plague Column in Vienna, Austria, is a memorial
to those who died during the plague.

Lester120/iStock/Getty Images

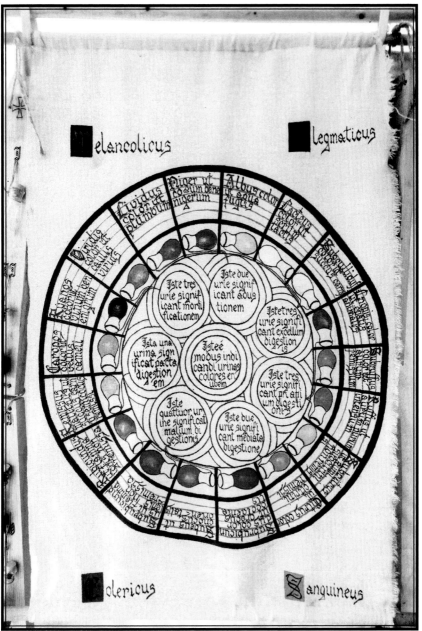

Chart used by medieval doctors to identify what was
wrong with a patient from the color of their urine

shoriclu/iStock/Getty Images

Christophe Boisvieux/The Image Bank/Getty Images

A statue of Saint Roch, a man who helped and comforted plague victims

Photos.com/PHOTOS.com>>/Getty Images

Christian flagellants punish themselves to atone for the plague in Europe.

Photos.com/PHOTOS.com>>/Getty Images

The fatal effect of
THE PLAGUE OF 1665.

Depiction of the Great Plague in London that took place from 1665 to 1666

Stamp featuring King Casimir III of Poland, the leader who tried to
protect the Jews in his kingdom from harassment during the plague

Veronika Roosimaa/iStock/Getty Images

duncan1890/iStock/Getty Images

A temporary hospital for patients in Hong Kong
during the Third Pandemic, in 1894

But most important of all, doctors studied samples of a sick person's urine. They believed that its color, smell—and, yes!—even its taste could reveal what was ailing a patient.

Urine chart used by doctors in the Middle Ages

Doctors would carry a urine chart with them when visiting sick patients. One medieval doctor became very famous for what he could tell from studying urine. So a friend of his decided to try to trick him. The man asked a woman who was pregnant for a sample of her urine. He gave it to the doctor, claiming it was his. After studying the urine, the doctor told his friend that quite soon he was going to have a baby!

If a patient was ill, it meant the four humors had become unbalanced. To learn why, doctors also studied the changing positions of planets and stars in the sky. If some of the planets, for instance, were close to or far apart from one another, that might be seen as a bad or dangerous sign. The outbreak of the plague was attributed to a dangerous alignment of Jupiter, Saturn, and Mars. The study of planetary positions is known as astrology. All medieval medical schools taught astrology. At some, students were required to spend three years studying it.

To prevent the plague, doctors advised patients to avoid bathing altogether. Why? A bath would open the pores on a person's skin and allow the poisonous plague air (called a *miasma*) to enter the body.

Astrology

Astrology is *not* the same thing as astronomy. However, it was taken very seriously during medieval times and even much later. Through astrology, physicians thought they not only could understand illness but also predict the future.

Today, some people still believe that the positions and movements of the stars and planets influence their daily lives. These predictions appear in daily horoscope columns in newspapers, in print and online.

Astrological birth chart

For people who already had the plague, bloodletting (blood draining) was the standard treatment. (That is if a doctor was willing to come anywhere near a plague victim.) By draining a certain amount of a person's blood, sickness would supposedly be released; the humors would get back into balance; and the person would be well again.

How was this blood draining done? A physician took a fleam (a small instrument with a sharp blade) and nicked a patient in a vein or artery. Blood came flowing out, and it was up to the physician to determine how much was enough.

Of course, bloodletting did nothing but cause the patient pain. Worse yet, if too much blood was lost, the patient would die.

Another medieval remedy was to give patients strong laxatives. This made them go to the bathroom a lot but did nothing to cure the plague.

Neither did lancing—piercing—an infected, painful bubo. What came out of it was not only disgusting and smelly but also released bacteria, infecting anyone who tried to clean up the mess.

For their wealthiest plague patients, doctors concocted expensive medicines. One was called theriac, made of mashed-up snakes and snakeskins as well as other ingredients. The poison in the snake was supposed to counteract the poison caused by the plague. Drinking powdered gold mixed into water or wine was another costly but ineffective remedy.

Occasionally, medical advice did help. Doctors could see with their own eyes that plague spread in crowded places like city streets. The air was "poisoned," they thought. So patients were told to stay isolated at home. That's what Pope Clement VI did. He lived in Avignon, France, not in Rome where the pope (the head of the Catholic Church) resides today. He remained cooped up in his bedroom with two fires kept burning, night and day. (The heat may have killed off any fleas on servants' clothing.)

Boccaccio and the *Decameron*

The writer and poet Giovanni Boccaccio (1313–1375) lived in Florence, Italy, during the time of the black death. He wrote a short story collection called the *Decameron*. In it, a group of ten people, all young and rich, flee the city to stay at a mansion in the countryside. There they hope to avoid the plague. Over the course of ten days, each of the ten tells a story; that accounts for the book's title. *Deka* means ten in Greek.

The *Decameron* was widely read when it first came out, and even today it is taught in many college literature classes.

The pope's doctors had no understanding of contagious diseases or the role of fleas in spreading the plague, but their orders worked!

Most people weren't rich enough to afford a doctor. But 40 percent of people with the bubonic plague *did* survive. There was also a very small

percentage of people who were lucky enough to never catch the plague. There was something in their bodies that made them resistant to it. However, "lucky" may not be the right word, since so many of these survivors ended up losing some or all of their loved ones.

CHAPTER 8
Why? Why? Why?

The big question was: Why had the plague come? What was the reason for so much death and suffering? Physicians pointed to natural causes—maybe a huge flood, volcano, or earthquake had let out the poisoned air that infected people.

The vast majority of people, however, were certain that somehow they'd made God angry and so they were being punished. At that time, almost everyone in Western Europe was Christian. They believed that God controlled everything that happened. Once God had brought a flood so great, it destroyed the world. Now, it seemed, God had delivered the plague. A writer named William Langland was sure of that. He said, "These pestilences were for pure sin."

Going to church was part of every Christian's life. There, they prayed to God—or to saints like Saint Roch—for forgiveness of their sins and for an end to the plague. Going way beyond this, some Christians took to beating their own backs with special whips. They hoped that punishing themselves might bring God's mercy and stop the

plague. They thought they were helping everyone else through their suffering. These people were known as flagellants (say: FLAH-jeh-lance).

During the Second Pandemic of the late 1340s, groups of flagellants—sometimes as many as five hundred—would travel, barefoot and wearing rags, from town to town, mostly in France, Germany, and Austria. They cried, sang, and tore out their hair. Their whips had nails on the ends so their backs soon turned bloody. Praying loudly, they walked through the streets. They always attracted a crowd; onlookers found these parades of pain thrilling. Sometimes they joined in the singing or kept shouting hysterically, "Save us!" Sometimes they even dipped handkerchiefs into the wounds of the flagellants, believing the blood was blessed.

If there were any Jewish people in the town, however, they stayed inside their houses, waiting anxiously for the flagellants to leave for the next town. They knew that, if given a chance, flagellants might kill them. And if not the flagellants, then during the years of the plague, it might be townspeople they saw every day.

In the Middle Ages, the Jewish population of Europe was very small. It is estimated that, at most, there were about one and a half million Jewish people. About one-third lived in

Spain and Southern France, where some Jewish communities had existed since the Roman Empire.

In the best of times, Jewish people were merely tolerated by the Christians they lived among. Often, they were restricted to living in a certain part of the city. To further set them apart, Jews had to wear a badge on their clothes—a patch of yellow fabric. It was a sign of dishonor. They were not allowed to own land or become tradesmen—blacksmiths, barrel makers, carpenters, and such. So although there were some famous Jewish doctors, most made their living by peddling goods, opening pawnshops, and lending money. If a farmer needed a new horse to plow his field, he might go to a Jewish moneylender. Just as banks do today, moneylenders were paid back the loan and also charged an interest fee. Having to pay this extra money made the Christians hate the Jews even more.

To the Christians, the Jews' greatest sin, however, was that they didn't believe Jesus was the son of God. In fact, for a thousand years, many Christians had accused Jews of being responsible for the death of Jesus. It is not so surprising, then, to learn that when the Second Pandemic of 1347 arose, blame was wrongly put on the Jewish people. A rumor started and spread rapidly that Jews were putting plague poison into village wells. That's all it took for murderous attacks on Jewish people to begin.

In 1348, eleven Jewish men from Savoy, in present-day France, were thrown into jail and tortured. Finally, one man named Agimet "confessed" before a panel of judges. He said that yes, the stories of poisoning were true: He had poisoned wells in Venice, Italy; Toulouse, France; and along the Mediterranean coast. Because of his forced confession, Agimet and the ten other men were burned to death.

From Savoy, copies of the confession were sent to other towns in France and Germany. In Basel, Switzerland, a special wooden house was built on a small island. There, all the Jews of Basel were locked up and burned alive. In Strasbourg, where there were almost two thousand Jews, all were burned at the stake. In other places, Jews were beaten or killed in their own houses. Some towns expelled the entire Jewish community, Christians stealing the possessions left behind.

Did anyone try to stop the violence against Jewish people? Yes, some. King Casimir III of Poland tried his best to protect all the Jews in his kingdom and even went further, inviting Jews from other

King Casimir III of Poland

countries to come live there. The result was that for hundreds of years, Poland had thriving Jewish communities. In Regensburg, Germany, 237 town leaders formed a band to make sure that Jews there remained safe.

One person above all tried to defend the Jews—Pope Clement VI. He respected Jewish learning. And he believed that Christianity and Judaism sprang from the same source—the belief in one all-knowing God. Clement VI wrote a paper called a "bull" that was distributed to churches.

A papal bull

In it, he came out condemning these false rumors, saying that Christians who believed them were wrong and had been "seduced by that liar, the Devil."

The pope made it clear that Jewish people had nothing to do with the plague. Common sense proved that—Jewish people were dying from the disease at the same rate as Christians. Pope Clement VI also asked priests to take in Jews and keep them safe. But that rarely happened. And terrified by all the death around them, common people were not willing to listen to common sense, so many innocent Jewish people continued to be killed.

CHAPTER 9
What Happened After?

By 1351, the plague had run its course. There were shorter waves of plague outbreaks over the next decades, but none were as destructive as the Second Pandemic. Then, for hundreds of years, the plague seemed to have gone underground, with one horrible exception: the

1665–1666 Great Plague epidemic in London.

Why did the Second Pandemic disappear? Scientists are trying to figure that out.

The world that survivors faced had been drastically changed. There were thousands of acres of abandoned fields and orchards, broken bridges, buildings falling down, and villages that seemed like ghost towns. There were so few craftspeople left who knew how to make shoes, barrels, cloth, tools, and horseshoes that prices for everything skyrocketed.

London (1665–1666): A Double Whammy

Over the course of seven months, the city of London, England, was hit with a major outbreak of the bubonic plague. To avoid getting sick, King Charles II fled from the city where, according to

records of the time, there was a total of 68,596 deaths!

Then, on September 2, 1666, a baker accidentally started a fire. For five days, it ripped through London, destroying 90 percent of the buildings in the city.

ıght expect, people had little ı the future. Evidence of their bleak ᴧ life shows up in the art of the post-ᴧ ears that often focuses on grim and terrifying representations of death. So many millions of people had been wiped out that not until the seventeenth century did the population of Europe reach its pre-plague size.

Drastic change, however, can benefit some people. This was certainly true for peasants. So many had died that those remaining had more power in dealing with the lords whose land they farmed. They no longer owed free labor to them. Nor were they legally bound to spend their lives at the manor. As a result, many decided to try their luck in a city. There, because the labor force had shrunk so much, workers demanded— and got—very high wages.

The life of women also improved; widows took charge of their dead husbands' farms, and they now could own land on their own. Instead of farming their land, more of it could be turned into pasture for cattle. Raising cattle was much easier than growing crops—and more profitable, too.

In cities, women had greater job opportunities. They could find work on the docks now. And they came to pretty much control the brewing industry! Also, slowly, the study of medicine began to change, no longer based on the mistaken teachings of ancient thinkers. Medical students learned about the human body by dissecting and studying it. They began to trust in scientific reason, not in astrological signs, for disease.

And though no one at the time could have known it, a great flowering of the arts and sciences was about to take place in Western Europe; Italy, to be specific. Within one hundred years, there began another one of those golden periods in history. It's called the Renaissance—in French, that means rebirth. It produced great artists and writers as well as scientific thinkers who first brought us into the modern world we know today.

Famous Renaissance artist Michelangelo

Timeline of the Plague

460 BC	Hippocrates is born
AD 129	Galen is born
541–544	The First Pandemic of the plague ravages the Byzantine Empire
1315	An Italian surgeon named Mondino De' Luzzi has a corpse dissected and later writes a book about human anatomy
1345–1351	The Second Pandemic of the plague overruns Europe, parts of Asia, and North Africa
1347	Caffa, a city on the Black Sea, becomes infected with the plague in a battle with Mongol soldiers
	In October, ships with infected sailors reach Messina, Sicily
1348	In January, the plague travels to Marseille, France, and on to England
	Boccaccio begins writing the *Decameron*
1349	The plague reaches Scandinavia
1665–66	The Great Plague epidemic in London, England
1855	The Third Pandemic of the plague originates in southwest China
1928	The antibiotic penicillin is discovered, which cures some once-fatal diseases

Timeline of the World

527–565	Justinian I rules over the Byzantine Empire
1066	William the Conqueror becomes king of England after the Battle of Hastings
1170	The University of Paris is founded
1215	The Magna Carta is signed in England, limiting the powers of the king
1271	Marco Polo begins his journey to Cathay (China)
1336	China suffers through terrible drought and famine
1337–1453	A series of conflicts known as the Hundred Years' War is fought over who has the right to rule France
1351	The game of tennis is first played in England
1492	Christopher Columbus crosses the Atlantic Ocean, from Spain to Hispaniola (present-day Haiti and the Dominican Republic)
1666	The Great Fire of London destroys much of the city
	Isaac Newton develops his theory of gravity
1796	Edward Jenner creates the first successful vaccine against smallpox
1885	Karl Benz invents the first true automobile
1929	The crash of the New York Stock Exchange sets off a ten-year economic collapse known as the Great Depression

Bibliography

Armstrong, Dorsey. *The Black Death: The World's Most Devastating Plague.* The Great Courses. Chantilly, VA: The Teaching Company, 2016. DVD.

Cantor, Norman. F. *In the Wake of the Plague: The Black Death and the World It Made.* New York: Simon & Schuster, 2001.

Hartnell, Jack. *Medieval Bodies: Life and Death in the Middle Ages.* New York: Norton, 2018.

Kelly, John. *The Great Mortality: An Intimate History of the Black Death, the Most Devastating Plague of All Time.* New York: HarperCollins, 2005.

Tuchman, Barbara W. *A Distant Mirror: The Calamitous 14th Century.* New York: Knopf, 1978.